GALILEE

*a collection of poems
by Peter Stiles*

POETICA CHRISTI PRESS

ISBN: 978-0-6484451-5-9

© 2025

Published by **Poetica Christi Press**
13 Alexandra Crt, Woori Yallock, 3139
Email : poetica@iprimus.com.au
Website : www.poeticachristi.org.au

Cover design and book layout by:
Wattle and Willow Books
www.facebook.com/wattleandwillowbooks

Cover photo © **Lorensz Stork**

Copyright for this book belongs to **Peter Stiles**.
Reproduction of poems from this book is allowable for non-commercial use
only but acknowledgement of authorship is required.

"Robert Frost once said 'a poem begins as a lump in the throat, a homesickness, a lovesickness. It finds the thought and the thought finds the words.' What emerges from the pages of *Galilee* is that, for Peter Stiles, poetic composition is essentially a homeward quest, a *nostos* compelled and sustained by a 'strong commitment to the life and teachings of Jesus Christ'. To quote a phrase from his 'Uluru Snapshots', these poems evince a 'gentle, crafted luminescence'. They are the work of a poet who does not retreat from the world's complexity but who discovers in its midst small, vital epiphanies of renewed hope and God's radiant love."

Dr Kathleen Riley, *author, scholar.*

"Peter Stiles' poems are gentle, humane, fragile in instances of memory of time, people and place – yet their beauty is also enduring, like the faith that lies at their heart. They pick up the little things that finally matter the most in life, experiences in many far-flung countries and cities across the world. These poems are rooted in a love of books and learning, without being bookish, for their true roots lie in the love of families and friends, both young and old, in the changing seasons of the Christian year, and the One who is its heart and soul."

The Reverend Canon Professor David Jasper,
DD FRSA FRSE, *Emeritus Professor – University of Glasgow.*

"*Galilee* reveals a poet for whom attention to the life of Jesus has transformed everyday life. Now he is 'trusting to silence and another way'; now he sees that 'October is opaline, as are wild duck feathers.' Peter Stiles' poems abide in a rich revelation of divine love."

Professor Kevin Hart, *Jo Rae Wright University Distinguished Professor in the School of Divinity, Duke University.*

"Peter Stiles anoints the discipline of poetry with divine grace and the balm of healing words: the shifting lightshows of the outback desert and majestic Uluru; the persistent call of indigenous culture across the ages; the riotous pilgrimage of the seasons with their intricate flora and fauna; the weakness of sickness and the onset of age; literary and musical giants who gently massage our inner being; the revelatory progress of the Christian calendar; Austin Farrer and C. S. Lewis, English theologians in fireside conversations; the retrieval of childhood, college, and family memories, quivering with emotion; and the cross of Christ, lifted high, above all, for all. A scintillating new collection of poems by Peter Stiles who reflects perceptively and compassionately upon our humanity and God's offer of transformative mercy to us all."

DISTINGUISHED PROFESSOR JAMES R. HARRISON,
Sydney College of Divinity.

"The 'Park Bench' is a poem in Peter Stiles' latest collection. In it he writes: 'She could hear his laughter as they worked'. I can hear laughter in Peter's work as I almost 'hear' the silence in some poems. Further, I can see the luminescence of light in the flight from Uluru and I can walk in each of Jesus' footsteps in 'Galilee'. Peter Stiles' poetry is evocative – intellectual and affective; generous and life purposing. I commend it to you."

DR PAUL BURGIS, *Principal, PLC, Sydney.*

*This collection of verse is dedicated to
my wife, Kerrie,
my children, Rachel (and Andie), Stephen (and Sara),
Andrew (and Hannah);
and my grandchildren, Matilda, Jemima, Barnabas,
Gabriel and Angus.*

Introduction

This collection of poems, my third, is entitled 'Galilee' because my worldview has been largely formed by a strong commitment to the life and teachings of Jesus Christ. To me, Jesus is the source of all that is good and worthy in this life (see Colossians, Chapter one). Hence my feeling for Him as expressed in the first poem with the same title.

Inevitably, in the complexity of human experience, a huge range of situations and ideas present themselves to the attentive eye of a poet. This poetic compendium represents the aggregation of so many observations, some casual and intriguing, others quite profound and moving. But that is what life is like, the keen observer picking up little things that might easily be passed over, while other matters are unavoidably significant. Such is the flow of daily living. Underneath it all, for me at least, Jesus Christ provides the measuring stick to assess meaning and value.

Some of the poems are derived from wonderful people I have known, books that I have read, or travels I have undertaken. Growing up in Tenterfield, in northern New South Wales, and then attending Armidale Teachers' College, were very formative experiences for me, as has been my married life with the addition of children and grandchildren. I have studied and taught overseas on a number of occasions, and it is not difficult to detect the love that Kerrie and I have for the United Kingdom and Western Canada. Some of our dearest friends live in these countries.

I have deliberately avoided sequencing the poems in any way because that is the way that recollection works, poetic ideas flooding in from all sides at different times. I hope that you enjoy these poems and that they create some resonances with your own life and experiences.

– Peter Stiles

Contents

Galilee	10
First Love	11
Easter Sunday	12
The Poet's Progress	13
Streams of Living Water	14
The Park Bench	16
Free from Crafting	17
October	18
Cutting	19
Waulking	20
Spring	21
Uluru Snapshots	22
Platypus	24
The Docket	25
Greenwich Hospital	26
Parramatta Postcards	27
Blue Gums	30
College Days	31
Spring and Poetry	32
'It is Raining'	33
Wedding at St. John's, Camden	34
Saddler Street, Durham	35
Sculpture at Barangaroo	36
Saint Francis College, Brisbane	37
Mount Athos	38
Trio for Advent	39
Lark Ascending	40
Epiphany Winds	41
Haiku for Uncle Innes	42
At the Carmelite Priory	43

The Library	44
Tribute to Ralph Vaughan Williams	45
Five Barley Loaves and Two Fish	46
Pilgrimage	47
Separated	48
The Poet	49
The Austin Farrer Biography	50
Austin Farrer	51
Matilda's Second Christmas	52
Blue Triangles in November	53
Chance Meeting	54
The Red Letterbox	55
Jacarandas in November	56
Reading the Nativity Narrative	57
On Hearing Malcolm Guite's Tribute to CS Lewis	58
Birthday Greetings	59
The Christmas Eve Picnic at Sandy Creek	60
The Morning Star	61
Avoca Beach	62
The Cross	63
One Day in Athens	64
For Waldo Williams	65
A Lament for Tea Pickers	66
Creek beds of Kindness	67
Acknowledgements	68
About the Author	69

Galilee

Through the gauze of history see this man,
   his dusty sandals, unkempt hair
      just touching the edges of a well-worn chitōn.
He feels the heat of summer on this rock-strewn road,
   often stubbing his toe or brushing thorn bushes.
The water from this well tastes brackish and warm
   and there are no gall oaks to shade him here.
His possessions are few, not even a staff
   to beat off savagery in man or beast.
Lunch is sparse, flat bread, dried fish and olives,
   no Roman banquet in this remote location.
He is on the edge of an empire,
   and fame and fortune bypass Galilee.
Tonight, he will sleep rough again in a field,
   or on a straw-filled mattress in a disciple's room.
This is a foreign place for him, so far from home,
   a land of shadows and brokenness.
But late at night, while others are asleep,
   his beard and hair vermilion in the moonlight,
      he is radiant in readiness for an alabaster jar
         of perfumed praise to anoint him.
For from his chosen poverty comes healing,
   and from his measured words comes peace.

First Love

In this New England farmhouse, I weigh each word,
    verses sparkling in a measured cup of meaning.
I believe and feel my fresh beliefs confirmed
    by a surge of peace, a gentle purity,
      like cool water dousing my face
        after a day near these golden wheat fields,
          tired after dispensing wisdom
            in my one-teacher, country school.
The nights are silent, barely a whisper,
    just the imagined rustle of kangaroos
      chewing ears of wheat in the top paddock.
Silent, and alone, far from family,
    the curtains move in the moonlight.

Tonight, I will sleep and dream of Galilee.

Easter Sunday

From concerning accounts of Covid cases
   we have sheltered, mixing fear and sadness,
      isolated in uncertainty.
Yesterday we walked the quiet streets
   in silence, avoiding others passing by,
      wan smiles of knowing, of dread.
An invisible enemy lurks in this season.
Holiday plans are cancelled,
   trains are empty, roads deserted, caravans idle.
The only realm of movement is the virtual world,
   the daily search for connection,
      for traces of relief.
Or this garden seat, this morning, where, with
   protected perspective, the natural world
      persists unhindered, safe and still.
For today,
   in the midst of a gentle incandescence,
      a new day burning,
         lies a beginning, this fresh hope.

The Poet's Progress

He shuffled some words and won a prize
  with a poem about fruit picking,
    a surprise for a country boy just out of school.
Quizzical, he had touched a vein of images,
  like the colours in an Arthur Streeton canvas.
He drew back in wonder from the notebook,
  his crabbed hand filling the tabula rasa.

Bearded and married he kept on writing,
  a young wife dancing before his thinking.
Now beyond the thick brocade of foliage,
  deep inside the darkness of life's branches,
    a stillness that assures, confirms
      there is a refuge from the glare,
        a place of safety in those branches.

He will write a poem about that.

Streams of Living Water

I

The perfection of water, dripping, seeping,
soaking me in this old summer shirt.
I hear it in rusty downpipes, trickling,
cars hissing through the slick on the road.
Distorting my vision, it runs down the windows.
It is wanting to turn, to turn into a stream,
and saturate this darkened room.
Outside on the brick path
I cup it in handfuls,
the taste of its puzzling coolness,
this water from blued, brooding clouds.
It runs down my cheeks,
down my neck, down my back.
I wipe it away like tears from my eyes.

Rainwater is a gift.

II

Slippery rocks at the top of this waterfall.
After flooding rains the moss grows freely,
fed each day by spray from the wind.
Be careful, others have fallen from here.
At this liminal point,
this stream from the mountains
plunges recklessly to the valley floor.
Behind safety rails, people stand and stare
at this ferment of fluidity.

In this peaceful room
I remember that day,
how the water kept coming,
delirious in volume and vibrancy.

I have witnessed whitewater insistence.

III

Purified water, soft and cool,
running through this sheltered room,
a stream that never ceases.
It stirs my days, it stirs my sleep,
gushing, gurgling near my feet
this lingering, liquid lullaby.
Illumined by streetlight
that glints on its surface
this bubbling balm beside my bed.

Wading through it is baptismal.

The Park Bench

Under a tree, sanded, smooth,
   screws tightened, no sharp edges,
     you could sit here in comfort, without splinters.
This restorative project was for her father,
   to inhabit the space his crafting hands
     had been in just two years before.
Two years of absence until now
   as she traced the grain as he had done,
     with the soothing aroma of treated timber.
She could hear his laughter as they worked,
   tools scattered across the workshop bench,
     her eyes delighted by father and daughter.
Her father's hammer, her father's saw,
   each movement took her to his side,
     for the moment her teenage pain subsiding.

Free from Crafting

for Jack Leax*

Voices from the past you do not want to hear
  are new bruises on your tired arms,
    weathered from bone-chilling winters
      in Upper New York.
Better to close them out like snowbound days
  and reach out to the one you really love,
    to the rocking chair she sits in
      day by day, past standing.
Years now since your students,
  earnest and bright-eyed,
    hung on your every metaphor,
      as you unpicked Walt Whitman and Thoreau,
        then had them copying these cadences.
Looking down as their hands moved across the page,
  you smiled at their modest beauty,
    their fairness, their pledge to be creative,
      to write a fresh and crafted image.
Fewer fresh images left in your hands now,
  but the woodlands still call,
    some mystery still untrammelled
      after years of solace seeking.
You are comfortable in your corner free from crafting.

---

* I wrote this poem some years ago. Sadly, Jack Leax (1943-2024) passed away with cancer at the end of last year. He taught English at Houghton College, Upper New York, for many years. He was one of the finest poets I have ever known.

October

Not a poetic word, *optimism*,
  neither are *optimal* or *opportunity*,
    but *October* needs some bright assonance,
      as the month of uplifted thinking,
        of sunshine, blossom and promise.
Today we saw the first flush of jacaranda,
  the usual mauve marker of November,
    carpeting the lawns and driveways.
And the heat today foreshadowed summer,
  when shadows are valued,
    like a dark room for ocular migraine.
Yesterday, in the Blue Mountains,
    two wild ducks, with sheen on their feathers,
      contentedly grazed in the long grass.
The allure of Advent brings colour
    to every living thing.
  October is opaline, as are wild duck feathers.

Cutting

His melodic lines had a cutting edge.
They cut through years and wing me to a town
   where a man gathers gentleness at a piano.
He is a refugee from the gory refuse
   of a day at the local meatworks.
Leaving his sharpened knife behind,
  in a metal locker, in a bare, cold room,
    he scrubs his hands, Brylcreems his hair
     and returns to town,
       to an ever-comfortable living room.
Now his crotchets and quavers
   cut to the bone,
     with unspeakable love in this
       New England town.

Waulking*

This film from nineteen forty-one,
   young women around a table, waulking,
     somewhere in the Outer Hebrides,
       gently kneading the tweed before them,
        singing an age-old Gaelic song.
Hands moving rhythmically,
  their voices lilting with promise,
    a chorus of youthful attention,
      spellbound by this outdoor moment.
At the top of the table
 an old lady smiles,
   her face lined with weathering.
She has seen this many times before,
  how joy fades into silence
    and waves lap at the rocky shore.
They are all gone now,
   and their headstones do not tell the story
     of a summer's day in Scotland
       as this old, archival footage does.

---

* Waulking is a step in woollen clothmaking that refers to the practice of cleansing the cloth to eliminate oils, dirt, and other impurities.

Spring

On the cusp of a seasonal change,
    turning back, turning to
        the sheltering warmth of simile,
            to stillness, silence and sunshine.

The promise embraces me,
    with colour at every corner,
        like removing concealing covers
            from a fresh green, rain-washed wicket.

There is trust in these liminal moments,
    a passage encountered before,
        I am hedged by a playful refreshment,
            ever true, ever young, evermore.

But the hottest July on record
    seeds my mind with troubling thoughts,
        will my grandson grow into summers
            with a fear of the heat, fire and drought?

In the garden a rainbow of lorikeets,
    a magnolia's magenta beauty,
        cool air flushes this vernal space –
            for the moment all is well.

Uluru Snapshots

Late Afternoon

From a distant vantage point
    we gaze attentively at Uluru.
It is washed with tonal inflections
    by a watercolourist seeking perfection.
With 'how the colour changes' on our lips,
    we are students in this desert studio.

Sturt's Desert Pea

Outside our hotel, in the rust-like soil,
    a sudden flair of blood-red colour.
The angular, black-eyed petals
    of this Australian icon catch my breath.
It longs to be photographed
    by every passer-by.

Mutitjulu Waterhole

This is a sacred place,
    an ever-constant source of water comfort.
The flaky arkose stone above
    sheds ancient stories,
        voices from the past
            rippling through deep time.

The Sounds of Silence

In this silence the desert waits.
A group of tourists passing through
    – dinner here, now, under an open sky.
Soon the enveloping silence
    smothers this slight disturbance.

The Flight

As we flew back from Uluru,
    a full moon shone on Broken Hill.
Thirty thousand feet below,
    pinpricking the landscape,
        a cluster of lights, the city at night.
My cabin window framed this scene
    of gentle, crafted luminescence.

Platypus

By Aunty Jess's house there was a stream,
   where platypus were frequently seen,
      rippling the water with their quiet cadenzas.
I was then a boy in a country town.
The world came to me in a rush,
   and a paddle of platypus
      never crossed my sight again,
         until I heard the news tonight.
They were just there,
   their presence not contested,
      lulling willows their canopy of welcome.
But now, a deliberate returning,
   platypus restored to a national park
      just south of Sydney.
Headline news for a city that seeks
   to triage a legacy of potential loss.

The Docket

The paper is crinkled, stained and torn,
    on a Sydney street, just after dawn.
It tells of a purchase, a modest amount,
    for chocolates, cheese, biscuits –
        a Saturday treat.
The store that they came from
    is just near this corner.
Imagine him buying
    these things for his daughter.
Him smiling, he sees her so rarely now,
    his asthma confining him
        indoors and wheezing.
Pollution a word he never used,
    in the country town
        where he was born.
From his farming background
    the concept of quality
        was for fruit, not for air,
            just purity there
                in those distant
                    New England mountains.

Greenwich Hospital

Every day that old building stands silent,
    cream brick and green-laced wrought iron verandas
        staring into the newness of its surroundings.
One day we had a picnic lunch
    in the stillness of that porch,
        your wheelchair tucked into a sunlit corner.
Behind those walls there are sacred memories
    of devout Sisters, their years of caring
        mellowing the flaking paintwork,
            and the stained cement paths.
The nearby trees, speechless but comforting
    are reserved in respect for the deeds of charity
        fostered in this place.

Parramatta Postcards

1

For simply stealing a bag of wheat,
   he came here as a convict,
      to endless gumtree ridges,
         and loneliness tearing at his heart,
            this silence like death after London.

But day by day this river flowed,
   a balm to his calendar of yearning,
      his wish to return to Essex,
         paeans ringing from his childhood.

Different voices here.
A Darug man fishing from his canoe
   with words he could not fathom,
      like nectar seasoning sadness.

With passing months it stilled his heart
   that the Darug man kept fishing,
      while he kept splitting sandstone.
It invited him into a deeper time
   by the Parramatta River.

2

After seven years he was released,
   Macquarie's act of mercy.
He met her in Sorrell Street one day,
   expanding his hopes in this growing town.
They were married at St. Patrick's Church
   in the light of incense and liturgy,
     few witnesses to this tradition
       but gumtrees like silent sentinels.
And the Darug man kept fishing
   on the Parramatta River.

3

His laden wagon slowly moved
   along the rutted roadways,
     backwards and forwards day by day
       into the bustling town
         with cedar logs and wheat and wool
           while he whistled himself into comfort.

On cold winter nights, Rose by his side,
   he stared into the crackling fire.
In his tidy cottage, his children asleep,
   he thought about the Darug man
     on the Parramatta River.

4

A picnic today at Parramatta Park,
    beside the opaque, silent water.
Blossom everywhere,
    and young chic bodies
        walking, running in the Spring sunshine.
I thought of my ancestor, centuries before,
    and the Darug man in his canoe.
I thought of how cruelty, pain and dispossession
    were conjured near this river,
        with its passive meanderings through time.

Blue Gums

Tall, whispering sentinels,
   huddling together in this sanctuary,
      spectral images of a forgotten landscape.
In this suburban street, sheltered and remote,
   this stand reminds me of a lost forest,
      a land unscarred by brick and tar.
Their height draws the stilled eye
   upwards
      to where cockatoos screech,
         dipping and contesting
            in the afternoon light.
We come here often now
   seeking to gain the wisdom
      of blue gums, while they remain.

College Days

for Neil

All jackets and ties in those days, sent back if we defaulted.
Just nineteen, Vietnam was calling
  as we hurried to lectures down corridors
    lined with inviting canvases.
We danced into tomorrow, where some were maimed
  but all were scarred by the cruelty of war so far removed
    from this gentle New England city.
The College on the Hill, commanding and solid,
    capturing the hearts of country boys
      and girls with straight pencil skirts
        and their sweet, demure smiles.
Our minds dabbled on many pages,
  a whirlwind of knowledge and desire.
Always church on Sundays, a Wesleyan refuge from raw edges
    and bland macaroni cheese.
The candle of faith burned quietly
  in this place of cathedrals and churches,
    the full, dulcet sound of the organ playing
      into the still, chilly night.
Remember frosty mornings,
  afternoons with duffle coats in Beardy Street,
    savoured cappuccinos.
And our hearts, so young, swung back to our families,
  just a train ride north or south, away from this season of promise.

Spring and Poetry

Just as this poem emerges word by word,
   surprising even me with hidden colours,
     so Spring arrives, and branches that were bare
       gradually display a flush of leaves.
This paper, made from trees,
  buds metaphors in quiet synergy.
The silent rhapsody of Spring and poetry.

> *'Let my teaching fall like rain*
> *And my words descend like dew,*
> *Like showers on new grass,*
> *Like abundant rain on tender plants'*
> *(Deuteronomy 32:2)*

It is raining.
There is wisdom in rain,
  a gentle, calm instruction
    for the many plants
      that blossom in my garden.
It soothes and beckons to them for brightness,
  to show strength in tenderness
    against the crushing strength of industry.

Year by year these azaleas have claimed
  a picturesque place in photos,
    more truth in their beauty
      than any passing figure,
        their vision of life so much bigger.

Late afternoon.
Sunlight glistens on the studio,
  lorikeets prattle in the trees,
    feeding on native nectar.
Every morning they come to our door for apple,
  neatly sliced for their insistence.

The sky is benign, the sun contests with clouds,
  a diorama of changing tones,
    an artist craving attention.

Wedding at St. John's, Camden

I
red lights, car-clagged roads
until the sun varnishes a
spire in the distance.

II
squint upwards through the morning light –
an infinity of matins and melodies
echoes from that timbered dome.

III
photograph the smiles and pastel tones
of wedding guests, transparent, and fixed
in a memory of youth and love.

Saddler Street, Durham

from a painting by Linda Vine

I know this street, also whitened with snow.
Walking the cobblestones to St. Chad's,
   I would pause to peer into Waterstones,
     or step inside,
       a welcome relief from the stinging cold,
         the constant comfort of rows and rows
           of books in mint condition.

You can just see the spire of St. Nicholas' Church
   from this doorway,
     a major presence for our lives in Durham.
Turning right from the bookshop,
   and up a slight rise,
      the solid, grand presence of the Cathedral,
        a solid, grand masterpiece resisting time.
Often, I lit a candle there against the darkening sky.

I can see beyond the borders of this canvas,
   my mind filling the circumference
     with treasured memories;
       like a palette of spilled colours,
         shaped by the laughter of children.

Sculpture at Barangaroo

I dance before the sunshine of this life,
   crafting my moments, thoughts scattered
     like seagulls across this spangled harbour.
Ferries plough their silent furrows towards the Quay.
We walk along the shoreline hand in hand,
   here our profiles sculptured by a photograph
     before this soothing angularity of steel.
Now a dark girl sweeps the path before us.
Turning, she smiles,
   an ageless acknowledgement of love.

Saint Francis College, Brisbane

Positioned by an ugly brewery,
    a contortion of pipes and industrial vulgarity,
        this Sabbath the college serenely slumbers.
In front of the chapel Saint Francis stands,
    gesturing to the silent lawns and gardens,
        manicured in their still devotion.
We, mere visitors, are drawn into this
    metaphor of peace, of purpose.

Trio for Advent

The first day of Advent.
Optimism blooms
  in Sydney's summer suburbs.
In our garden
  a tumbling trio of wild rabbit kittens.
Assured of their safety
   they are a Christmas pantomime,
    startling our smiles
      with their gentle presence.

Tenderness comes in threes.

Lark Ascending

There is a space between desire
   where sound filters thoughts
     and pure landscapes shine.
A bird, a sky, a summer,
   the rolling English hills
     and dulcet memories.
The Yorkshire Dales that day.
A violin notes my reverie,
   with glimpses of a stream,
     a Roman road, a foursome,
       in silence, then in awe.
The lark ascends
   in traceries of flight,
     catching my breath with song
       then out of sight.

Mount Athos

for Scott Cairns

Searching for a place where life is prayer,
   where hesychia endures through night and day,
     and prayer gives way to sleep and then to prayer,
        I read your book, memorable Mount Athos moments,
           mystérion ever before your thoughts.

In the hard walks and the cold nights,
   you found a brilliance in the darkness,
     a balm for your bruised travelling,
       uncovering monastic treasures for the soul.

In this Lenten light I long to learn
   where I can find that pilgrim's place of peace,
     a mountain in this mind of sighs
       to lift my hungry heart to things divine.

Epiphany Winds

morning

        seagulls, hovering,
        waiting to swoop on a
        fleck of divine grace.

afternoon

        cottage against the lake.
the rattle/knock/rage of January winds,
  pale skies, and a smearing rain.
  In each room a family member reads,
  warmed by silent thoughts
  (storm wind outside/ stillness within).

evening

        laughter, and the
        letter tiles of Scrabble.
        near midnight, all asleep,
        the only word a constant, cradling wind.

Haiku for Uncle Innes

The red kimono
passes, his steady eyes on
a finer text of love.

At the Carmelite Priory

Writing out of the moment,
    writing out of the stillness,
        green brocaded with green,
            slender tree trunks reaching to the blue.

In the distance birds trill,
    air touches the branches like a presence,
        to and through the foliage it moves,
            caressing creation with soft hands.

I relax into the features of such finesse,
    the lengthening lines of afternoon light,
        the sunlight moving to the horizon,
            drawing me towards tomorrow.

I try not to live in my mind at the moment,
    but stay anchored here, fully attentive.
        In the distance the dull roar of traffic,
            the world outside this gentleness.

I am trusting to silence and another way,
    the unearthly steadiness of solitude.
        In a field nearby cows follow each other,
            making their way to the milking shed.

The sun is setting.

The Library

This house covets books,
   arranged volumes, row after row,
      mustering clusters of thought and endeavour,
         fertile minds between these covers.
Appetites change, our tastes, our passions,
   gathered by author their spines, the stages
      when Austen, Jhabvala, Gaskell, Lewis,
         were measured, deft treasures
            through quiet days and evenings.
Some best remembered, the light, the song,
   the age we considered Jamesian gems,
      our heartbeat slowing in crafted stillness.
Places unknown become real, become clear,
   the London of Dickens, and Wessex air,
      streets, lanes and fields from this sitting room chair.
But we keep them all, these seasoned markers,
   glimpses of insight, of growth, of knowing,
      lexical markers to mellow our moments.
Solzhenitsyn looms large, his sober tomes,
   refreshing nightmares of book-burning Marxists,
      and Siberian, limitless landscapes.
Here Berry's covers, a more recent lustre,
   through our thoughts flow Kentucky summers,
      and the wisdom of Marilynne Robinson.
Slim volumes of poetry confetti the shelves,
   a palette of bright verbal colours,
      Herbert and Hopkins amongst many others.
This library is a place of ease,
   a refuge for bibliotherapy.

Tribute to Ralph Vaughan Williams

Fantasia on a Theme by Thomas Tallis
    evokes the inexplicable.
Reeling, young composers walked
    the streets of Gloucester after its debut
        trying to capture through that night
            the meaning in its acuity,
                its touching tonalities.
Something like a blind
    suddenly opened to sunlight.

That autumn concert in England
    is clear to me today.
But as I listen to this recording,
    the message in these cadences,
        sonorous and spacious,
            still evades me,
                teasing me into reflection.

Five Barley Loaves and Two Fish

From a place of limits and yearning,
    with barley loaves, fish and heart drumming,
      he pushed to the front of the surging crowd,
        this mother's precious, blue-eyed boy.
There the teacher stood, followers beside him.
Astounded, he gave them his lunch when asked,
    the fish he had caught that morning gone
      with the oven fresh loaves, a mother's love.
But the teacher was kind, soon tears became smiles.
In the right hands,
    five and two become thousands.

Pilgrimage

I long to walk Saint Cuthbert's Way,
   to follow in his footsteps to the glassy sea
     and cross the rocky shallows to
        Lindisfarne, that Holy Island.
There to sample liminal grace,
   the space where earth meets heaven;
     that gentle place reserved for souls
        retreating from complexity.
An ageing pilgrim with aching knees
   I foresee the challenge,
     like kneeling for evening vespers,
        satisfaction in the seeking.
The path unfolds before my mind,
   the beckoning, green hills,
     the cool breeze and the coast beyond.
Body and soul must push through pain
   and train for this forthcoming Spring,
     this Spring of saintly promises.

God grant me the way.

Separated

for Ann

Today we met to celebrate her life,
    her death still fresh to our thinking.
With prawns, oysters, salmon slice,
    we recounted our fondest memories.
Family photos brought the past alive,
    that Christmas in Saint Alban's
        when the lake froze, or,
            visits to Sydney, her colourful quilting
            casting patterns into cloth.
We laughed and ate and laughed again
    positioning her in our prayers, this room,
        here with this beachscape she loved so much,
        the place of her childhood.

Sea mist lingers in the air like tears.

The Poet

   Spades of time for thimbles
     of syllables, snatched during
        daylight glimpses,
           like a thirsty man
              ringing water from
                a wet towel
                    before the midday sun.

The Austin Farrer Biography

*"for Stephen on your birthday '89,
with much love from Margaret"*

Some friendships leave behind just traces.
Birthday wishes with fading ink in front of
   the Farrer biography from decades ago,
      and a bookmark stating, 'Rejoice in the Lord'.
Few clues, but many assumptions,
   a devout couple, surely, I imagine them
      kneeling before the altar,
         light streaming through English leadlight.

Austin Farrer

A life lived in other's thoughts, your words
  grazing on a legacy of theocratic gestures,
    finding a space to make your own assertions,
     reportedly, then, 'a hawk among sparrows'.
An unstartled life of bookish commitment,
   secure in your calling, secure in your faith,
    content with the mantle of mentor, Don and author.
Your writings make your ideas clear,
   personal feelings evading precision,
    surely a deliberate decision.
Your friendship with Jack Lewis leaves blank spaces,
   the unrecorded teas, walks and conversations,
    just participation in his marriage and his funeral.
Like all good friends and teachers you deflected,
   valued more in influence than impression.

Matilda's Second Christmas

There's a Bethlehem brightness in Matilda's smiles,
    that makes all preparations seem right.
        Her own Advent joys are
            a plain teddy bear,
                wrapping paper to tear,
                      decorations catching the afternoon light.
Touched by the music of Christmas love,
    she dances to every tune:
        the humming of carols,
           the clash of toy cymbals,
                she nods in delight at the sounds in the room.
With her hands outreached for the angel on the tree,
    our hands reach out for Matilda.

Blue Triangles in November

Three blue butterflies above the bonnet,
   a frenzied tapestry of interweaving colour,
     the magnetism of mutual attraction
        sweeping them upwards into
          the afternoon light,
            like Advent tinsel.

Chance Meeting

for Ann

Fifty years ago in May,
    a woman hugged me in the street
        in Eastwood, near a fabric shop,
            surprising me with her youthful charm.
Fired in my memory
   and glazed with brightness
      that brief encounter spun a potter's wheel
         between two couples,
            continents apart,
                for all these ensuing decades.

The Red Letterbox

I was twenty, gentle and bookish,
    fresh out of college and with youth-spun ideals.
Opening that red letterbox in Gunnedah
    my hands trembled when I saw
        the foreboding, official letterhead,
            stern in austerity and purpose,
                like a hammer falling in a courtroom.
Before my eyes dense jungles loomed,
    the whirl of 'copters,
        and smoke and gunfire.
A barrel roll could seal my days,
    explode my dreams like a mortar shell.
I remember the moment with crystalline vision,
    the driveway, the fenceposts, the red letterbox,
        blood red on that still afternoon.

Jacarandas in November

This one poem captures those weeks in November
    when memories seep in from Decembers.
The recurring sense of anticipated jingles,
    the colours and contours of Christmas.
Jacarandas brocade the suburbs I drive through,
    like diary markers, mellowing moments.
They shower the streets with pastel promise,
    paving the way for Advent.

Reading the Nativity Narrative

Again and again we come back to these pages,
   seeking for wisdom within.
We ponder, conjecture, read and review,
   unpicking each passage with care,
     attentive, with treasures, so as not to disturb
     canonical texture and truths.
In the Hebrew section some episodes warn,
   reflecting contemporary pungency.
But the Nativity narrative washes darkness away,
   unveiling a canvas of colour;
     the joyful section of this gallery,
       vibrant with splashes of promise.

On Hearing Malcolm Guite's Sonnet in Tribute to CS Lewis

It was at the dinner table we heard your poem,
The timbre of your voice a welcome guest,
Clearly paying tribute to the man,
Remembering when he was sadly laid to rest.
Lewis lived a humble life but worthy,
Focusing on the gifts that he was given.
Your sonnet picks up those years of deep devotion,
The many ways his pen and voice had striven
To engender love for God in a darkening world,
To open insights on the richest pearl.
In every way your poem is deeply moving,
Assuring us of the value of words well chosen,
Of passion for a life acutely soothing
To the troubled hearts that unbelief is bruising.
Keep writing Dr. Guite and keep on showing
That poets committed to God are well worth knowing.

Birthday Greetings

for my book launch, November, 2022

Only time and space divide us, Jack,
   those fickle elements of life that smudge
      our desire to know, to bond, converse,
         as you did with your Oxford friends.

The Lamb and Flag is open again,
   pint glasses clinking in the cheerful chatter,
      festooning the street as if you were there
         with your pipe and sonorous modalities.

The November chill does not subdue
   Charles Williams' wit or Tolkien's tones
      as you cluster around a dark oak table,
         discussing myths and the dartboard fable.

We salute you, Jack, almost sixty years
   since you walked those streets in your faded tweed,
      but your strong voice lingers, your words impart
         wisdom today, as our bookshelves display.

The Christmas Eve Picnic at Sandy Creek

a childhood memory

A family picnic beside a creek,
    just outside our country town.
The children paddle in shallow water,
    knowing there are yabbies
        under those nearby rocks.
With picnic hamper and rug spread wide
    the parents savour the summer sun
        filtered through the tall gum trees.
Those sentinels hug the hillside,
    basting the morning with eucalyptus,
        the welcome aroma of summer.
There is a stillness deep inside that foliage,
    a silence steeped in promise.
Now, through the undergrowth,
    the restless, rustling surge of love.

Tomorrow all will be brilliance.

The Morning Star

for Angus

The universe is vast, defying comprehension,
    no clear edges yet have been defined.
Each year more galaxies are fashioned,
    astronomy capturing images from
        new stars light years distant.
Like dark dreams these images can trouble
    even more the puzzles of human life.

But one morning star, one glorious star
    burns brightest, sure and steady
        by its presence in our crowded skies.
With asteroids aflame,
    and protostars colliding,
        with black holes conjuring fear
            of time and space, it shines.

Here is a star to look to every daybreak,
    a star that comforts even the smallest child,
        softly beaming through the window
            of his city bedroom as
                he nestles with his favourite teddy bear,
                    cradled in the promise of a nativity,
                      that is pitted against the perils of infinity.

Avoca Beach

The magnetism of margins can be seen
    in the many figures gathered on this beach.
Family and athletic mingle as one,
    rushing in and out of the crested breakers.
Children play in the towel-flicked sand,
    their satisfied voices seashore muffled,
        as waves maintain their constant motion.
In this heat all elements lull,
    the alchemy of sun, surf, sand.
The summer daylight gently lingers,
    evaporating time and expectations.

That night, from our bedroom, rich in darkness,
    we can hear the sea, that relentless soothing,
        anointing us with liminal luxury.

We sleep soundly.

The Cross

The carpenter's son was used to nails
  being driven into timber,
    keeping his hands well clear
      as cedar, cypress, pine and oak
        were shaped to useful settings.

Nails driven through wrists is a different issue,
  a scream against fine grain,
    a fissure in finesse, a brutal act,
      timber to see an innocent man be slain.

But this tree, abashed, now centuries old,
  again and again has blossomed,
    amassing a glorious canopy of colour.
In defiance of evil,
  the Cross became our rich and living arbour.

One Day in Athens

I barely remember the Parthenon,
   as impressive as it was,
      and the Moussaka at lunch was ordinary
         compared to my wife's delights.
But I do recall the taxi ride,
   careening through narrow streets,
      like a vendetta against tranquillity,
         burning memory with caustic fright.
Dazed by this day, we almost then
   missed our ongoing London flight.

For Waldo Williams

after reading 'Between Two Fields'

Between two days I fell into your verse,
   the view from Parc y Blawd has held my gaze,
     of men with pitchforks quietly heaping hay,
       under an ever-changing bright Welsh sky,
         birdsong in flowering gorse and ragged hedges.

A voice I know is simmering in these verses,
   the one who is always near in wind and silence,
     his presence fills the clouded days and clearer,
       and harbours in these syllables and words,
         touching a common bond from poem to poem.

A Lament for Tea Pickers

Each day I drink the tea that you have picked,
   carefully packaged brands that are well known.

Sad that your aching poverty becomes
   fine China comfort to so many,
     I pray that kindness speak at last
       for long, long days on hillsides
        void of female comforts,
         and homes where tables, bare,
           groan with gnawing hunger and despair.

The pity of the pickers' plight
   troubles my every teacup.

Creekbeds of Kindness

for Carolyn

Stoney Creek near Tenterfield, for picnics as a child.
Afternoons spent yabbying,
   or sailing paper boats in rock-strewn currents.
Then tomato sandwiches, my father's sweet delight.
A quiet, sun-soaked creekbed of kindness.

All my life the silence of Bluff Rock
   towers in my memories, and this creekbed
     rippling, shelters warmest thoughts
       of aunts and uncles, fine partners
        in these creekbeds of kindness,
          like jolly Uncle Mervyn, the bustling farmer.

Such creekbeds of kindness
  have rippled down the years.
I sit beside them often with my family,
  tracing their precious presence
    in other moments when we celebrate,
      and laugh and linger over wine and lunch.

And I remember the sand, silence and sandwiches.

Acknowledgements

Grateful acknowledgement is made to the editors of the following publications, in which some of the poems first appeared.

'Sculpture at Barangaroo', published in *Love's Footprint*, edited by Maree Silver and Leigh Hay, Poetica Christi Press, Melbourne, 2019.

'Easter Sunday', published in *Joy in the Morning*, edited by Janette Fernando and Maree Silver, Poetica Christi Press, 2020.

'Cutting', published in *The Curator* (online), 2022.

'Galilee', published in *Transformation*, edited by Maree Silver and Janette Fernando, Poetica Christi Press, 2022.

'The Poet', published in *Quadrant*, January/February, 2023.

'Pilgrimage', published in *Luft Anthology (Poetry, Prose and Art)*, Mounted Ari, 2023.

'Uluru Snapshots', 'Wedding at St. John's, Camden', and 'Pilgrimage', published in *Journeys*, edited by Maree Silver and Leigh Hay, Poetica Christi Press, 2023

'The Red Letterbox', joint winner of the *Studio Poetry Prize*, in Studio, Number 159, 2023.

'College Days', 'First Love', 'The Park Bench', 'October', 'Greenwich Hospital', Saint Francis College, Brisbane', 'Trio for Advent' and 'At the Carmelite Priory', in *Studio*, 2023.

'Mount Athos', 'Lark Ascending', and 'Tribute to Ralph Vaughan Williams' in *Quadrant*, 2023.

About The Author

Dr. Peter Stiles graduated from Macquarie University with a Bachelor of Arts and then a Master of Arts in English Literature. During those years he was pursuing a teaching career in NSW government primary schools (having graduated from Armidale Teachers College, where he won the Poetry Prize). In 1979 he transferred to teaching English in secondary schools, and subsequently became Head of English in two state high schools. He then undertook a Master of Education degree at the University of NSW.

After pursuing theological studies at Regent College, Vancouver, in 1987, he decided to undertake a Doctorate in Literature and Theology, initially at Durham University, and then at the University of Glasgow. Peter then chose to move into the private school sector, where he had executive roles at two leading private schools. Since 2016, Peter has been lecturing at Excelsia University College, in Pennant Hills, for several years in the role of Senior Lecturer in Education. He is also a permanent member of the Academic Board at Excelsia.

Peter's first collection of verse, *Trumped by Grace*, was shortlisted for The Australian Christian Book of the Year in 2017. His poetry has been published widely in Australia and the United States. His second collection of verse, *Surprised by Jack*, was published in 2022. It concerns the life and work of C. S. Lewis and also contains a section of poetic reflections on life in the Blue Mountains, west of Sydney.

www.ingramcontent.com/pod-product-compliance
Lightning Source LLC
Chambersburg PA
CBHW062043290426
44109CB00026B/2716